Look What You Can Make With

Tubes

Edited by Margie Hayes Richmond

Photographs by Hank Schneider

Highlights for Children, Inc.
Honesdale, Pennsylvania

Designer
Lorianne Siomades

Contributors
Maureen Murray Casazza

Kathy Murray Pietraszewski

Margie Hayes Richmond

Lorianne Siomades

Edna Harrington

Olive Howie

Matthew Stockton

Highlights for Children
PO Box 18201
Columbus, Ohio 43218-0201
Printed in China through Colorcraft Limited, Hong Kong

Library of Congress Cataloging-in-Publication Data
Look what you can make with tubes / edited by Margie Hayes Richmond ; photographs by Hank Schneider.—1st ed.
[48]p. : col.ill. ; cm.
Summary : Toys, trinkets and other terrific craft ideas all from cardboard tubes.
ISBN 978-1-56397-677-3
1. Paper sculpture—Children's literature. 2. Handicraft—Children's literature.
[1. Paper sculpture. 2. Handicraft.] I. Richmond, Margie Hayes. II. Schneider, Hank, ill. III. Title.
745.54—dc20   1997   AC   CIP
Library of Congress Catalog Card Number 96-80396

First edition, 1997
Books in this series originally designed by Lorianne Siomades
The text of this book is set in Avant Garde Demi. Titles are set in Gill Sans Extra Bold.

20 19 18 17 16 15 14

Getting Started

This book is crammed full of fun, easy-to-make crafts that each begin with a cardboard tube. You'll find a wide variety of things to make, including holiday decorations, gifts, toys, and games.

Directions

Read all the directions for each craft before you start. Big, beautiful photographs make following the step-by-step directions a snap. This really is a time when "a picture is worth a thousand words." The picture will help you better understand how to make the craft and will inspire you to make yours beautiful and unique. When we tell you to "decorate," that means use paint, crayons, markers, or whatever you like to make your craft colorful and personal. Let your imagination soar, but always remember that paint and glue need time to dry!

Work Area

It's always best to protect your clothing and work surface. So you may want to wear a smock or apron. A parent's or older sibling's old shirt works nicely, too. Simply trim off or roll up the sleeves. Next, cover the floor, table, or counter top where you will work with paper. Old newspapers are great. Or you can cut up large brown-paper grocery bags and tape a few together. Some craft-makers use old worn-out sheets. Remember to clean up when you're done!

Materials

Start now to save and store cardboard tubes. Enlist the help of your friends and relatives, especially around the December holidays. Gather supplies and put them into a box or basket. The picture below shows most of the basic supplies you will need. Add others as you think of them. There is a list of materials for each craft. Get those things before you start. If you intend to make only one of the crafts, compare the directions and the materials list. You may not need all the items that are listed.

Very Important

You'll find that many crafts have ideas for three or four different crafts based on one basic idea and set of directions. Plus every craft is presented with a *More Ideas* section. You'll also think of new ideas of your own once you get rolling. So browse through these pages, choose a craft, and have some creative fun. Before you know it, you'll be exclaiming, "Look what I *made* with cardboard tubes!"

Clowns, Cadets, and Cowboys

You can make a whole cast of cardboard characters. And they don't all have to begin with "C." The characters you can make are limited only by your imagination.

You Will Need:

- cardboard tubes
- cardboard or foam board
- glue
- scissors
- paint or markers
- construction paper
- various items for decoration: pompons, yarn, plastic eyes, rickrack, twine, chenille sticks

More Ideas

How about making a cowgirl, cook, or captain (for more "C" words). Or try a butler, a police officer, a nutcracker, an astronaut, or a self-portrait.

If you celebrate Christmas, make an entire nativity scene. Follow the basic directions to make Mary, Joseph, shepherds, and Wise Men. Can you figure out how to make a baby from a small tube held horizontally? For a real challenge, make a crib. Glue two small tubes together in an X shape. Then use two more to make another X. These will be the crib's legs. Make the bed part from cardboard. Look at the raft on page 14 for general ideas of how you might make a stable.

To Make the Basic Character

1 Choose "who" you want to make and select a tube for the body. We used parts of wrapping paper tubes for our characters. Any size tube will work. Maybe you'll want to make characters of several different sizes.

2 Plan how you want to dress your character. Sketching it out first might be helpful. Gather all your costume needs and get to work. Try pretending you are a toy designer.

3 Think of the tube in three parts—head, body, and legs. All you have to do to form the legs is draw a line from the bottom of the tube. Stop the line at a point less than halfway, but more than one-third of the length of the tube—unless you want a character with extra-long legs. Of course, you won't draw in the legs until you've painted the tube or covered it with paper.

So stock up on cardboard tubes of all sizes. Your friends are going to want to make a crowd of their very own creations.

To Make the Clown

We covered our clown's body and legs with yellow construction paper and then drew in the line to form the legs. Decorate two small tubes for arms. Look at our picture to judge where to glue them on to the "body" tube. Attach big feet made from foam board or cardboard. Decorate your clown. We used construction-paper hands, ears, mouth, and hat; plastic eyes; a pompon nose; and yarn hair. Isn't he funny looking!

To Make the Cadet

His uniform is gray construction paper wrapped around the tube. The jacket features strips of white paper highlighted with gold foil. The buttons are metal fasteners. Ask an adult to help you make the holes. Put a dab of glue by each hole to help secure the metal fastener once it is inserted. Gold garland epaulets and cord trim finish off the jacket. We used foam-paper shoes and made a hat from construction paper and foam paper. Add some gold cord, an aluminum-foil shield, and a chenille-stick plume to the hat. Draw on facial features, and you're ready to march.

To Make the Cowboy

His face and hair are done with black pen and colored pencil. His shirt is red construction paper and the pants are denim, of course. Belt, boots, and hat are made from foam paper, but lightweight cardboard will work just as well. Don't forget to decorate the boots before you put them on. A twine lasso and a gingham kerchief are the finishing touches. Howdy, "pardner."

Shaggy Dog

Make a "pet-able" toy for yourself or to give to a friend.

You Will Need:

- cardboard tube
- cardboard egg carton
- paint
- yarn
- glue
- various items for facial features: plastic eyes, buttons, felt, construction or foam paper

1 Cut two sets of two connecting cups from a cardboard egg carton for the dog's front and back feet. Cut two individual cups for the head and tail. Paint them.

2 Use a cardboard tube for the body. Glue it to the sets of feet. Glue on the head and tail cups. Cut pieces of yarn for hair and glue in place. Then decorate the head. We used plastic eyes, a button nose, and foam-paper ears.

More Ideas

Make a purring kitty or a poodle using ribbon curls instead of yarn.

Wind Chime

Delight in the sounds of a gentle breeze.

You Will Need:

- cardboard tube
- paint or paper
- string, yarn, or ribbon
- seashells

1 Choose a tube for your chime and decorate it. We painted ours, giving it a "marbled" look. Wouldn't gluing on sand and other natural seashore materials be nice?

2 Punch holes near the bottom of the tube. Thread lengths of string through the holes and the shells. (You'll be surprised at how many shells have natural holes.)

More Ideas

Instead of shells, tie on pretty, shiny metal buttons.

Turn the chime into a room freshener. Instead of shells, tie on cinnamon sticks and tiny net bags filled with spices.

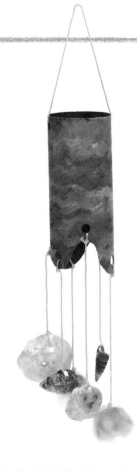

Tubie the Robot

Aren't there times when we all wish we had a robot of our own to help out with chores or just to keep us company? You can make your own robot—figuring out those magic powers might be tougher!

You Will Need:

- cardboard tubes
- box, such as a small cereal or cake-mix box
- paint or construction paper
- scissors
- glue
- various items for decoration: felt, glitter, beads, chenille sticks

More Ideas

Hide a small portable radio on or near your robot. When someone approaches, turn on the music to surprise them. Or better yet, use a tape recorder and make a tape using your "robot voice" to greet visitors.

Dress yourself as a robot for a costume party or Halloween and take your "robot" along in the parade. You might want to attach a curved strip of cardboard to the head for a handle.

1 Decide how big you want your robot to be and choose cardboard tubes. A section of a sturdy wrapping paper tube works best for the body. Decorate the tube. We made our robot look like silver metal and decorated his control panel with assorted buttons, beads, glitter, pieces of felt, and strips of masking tape that were painted red.

2 Choose and decorate tubes for the robot's legs and arms. Cut two 1" slits across from each other at the top of each leg. Looking at our picture will help you determine where to put these slits.

3 You can make hands and feet from cardboard tubes, too. We cut a 4" section from the sturdy tube and then cut it in half to make our feet. For hands, we cut two 1" rings from a tube and then cut out a ½"-1" piece. Decorate and attach the hands and feet.

4 Attach the legs by slipping the body into the slits. For extra security, apply glue or tape. We attached the arms with metal fasteners so they can move. (You'll need to punch holes in the body and in the arms first.)

5 Decorate the box for the head. We used beads, felt, and glitter. Our eyes are an old contact-lens case with black circles and "glass" buttons attached. Then we added some chenille-stick antennae.

Tag-Along Tubes

Decorating tubes and then stringing them together makes a great toy or room decoration to hang on the wall or across a window or top of a doorway. Be sure you have lots of tubes for this one.

You Will Need:

- cardboard tubes
- paint, crayons, markers
- yarn, ribbon, or thread
- paper punch
- construction paper
- plastic straws
- various items for decoration

1 Decide what kind of tag-along you want to make and how long you want it to be. Obviously, the longer you make it, the more tubes you will need. Gather your tubes and be sure you have plenty of thread, yarn, or ribbon. Fishing line is another good choice because it's so strong.

2 Cover your tubes with paint or paper. Punch a hole at each end of each tube. The holes should be about ½" in from each end of the tube, and they should be directly across from each other. It might help to make one hole and then draw a straight line from it to the other end on the outside of the tube. That will show you exactly where to make the second hole. Naturally, the tube for the front (or head) and the end (or tail) of your tag-along will need only one hole.

3 Cut lengths of yarn to be used to tie your tag-along pieces together. (The number of lengths of yarn you need will be one less than the number of tag-along pieces you have.) Make sure to cut the yarn at least an inch longer than you want the distance between your tag-along pieces to be. For example, if you're making the train and you want 2" between the cars, cut your yarn into lengths of at least 3". You'll see why in Step 4.

More Ideas

Decorate your tubes, tie them together, and hang them vertically. Make lots of them and hang like streamers to decorate for a party. Or make curtains like the bead curtains that were popular in the 1970s. A grown-up can show you what we mean.

Decorate a sturdy paper plate, punch holes around the edge, and tie on four or five tag-alongs. You've got a great moveable mobile.

Instead of train cars, decorate each tube with a letter of your name. Hang this nameplate on your door. Make one for a friend.

If you're really ambitious, make a number line of 1 to 10 or an alphabet row for a preschooler.

Read the directions before you begin. There are some slight variations that you need to be aware of early in the creative process.

4 Use the yarn to tie your tag-along pieces together. Thread the yarn into each hole and tie carefully, making secure knots. It's these knots that require the extra yarn. If the lengths of yarn are too short, you'll find it's almost impossible to tie them. In fact, it might be smart to make lengths of really long yarn and then cut off the extra once you've tied the knots. Another helpful hint is to dip the ends of the yarn in glue to make the threading process easier.

5 Cut a length of a plastic-drinking straw for each piece of your tag-along. The straw should be about an inch shorter than the tag-along piece. Affix this straw to the top of the tag-along tube. (The top is the opposite of where you punched the holes.) Use strong glue and/or tape. Thread a long length of yarn or fishing line through the straws. It should be at least 18" longer than your tag-along when it is all stretched out.

To Make the Train

Add details to your decorated tubes. We used construction paper for our sets of wheels. Cardboard, foam board, buttons, or milk lids will make great wheels, too. The cab of our engine is made from cardboard with a foam-board top. And the grill is a section of a tube. The smokestack is the top of an old marker. When your train is done, have someone help you tie each end to something sturdy—a chair, a doorknob, or even bedposts. Make sure the yarn or fishing line is taut. Now "guide" your train on a journey.

To Make the Snake

When you decorated your tubes in Step 2, did you make a colorful, silly snake like ours? Or did you choose a specific kind of real snake to make? Nature's colors and patterns are really cool, too. Don't forget to add eyes and a tongue. We just wanted our snake to lie on the "ground," so we didn't do Step 5. You can decide which way you want to do yours. Either way, your snake can slither along.

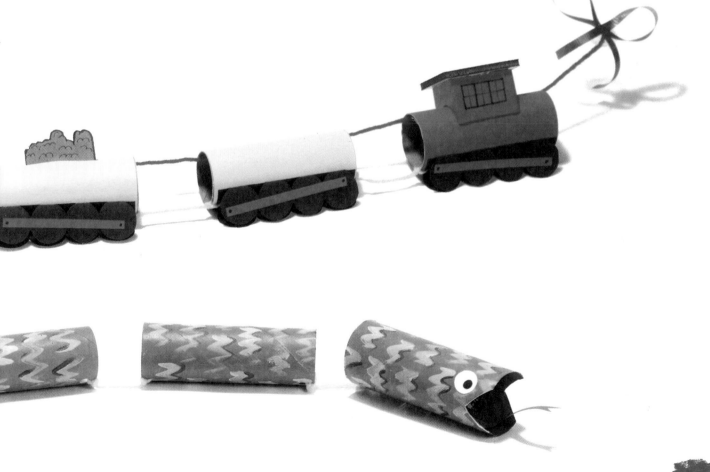

Finger Puppets

Get ready to wave your magic wand, play ball, or clown around. With finger puppets like these, you can "be" whatever you choose.

You Will Need:

- bathroom tissue tube
- colored paper
- paint, crayons, markers
- scissors
- glue
- various items for decoration: yarn, rickrack, fabric, chenille sticks, felt, netting, sequins

1 Decide which puppet you want to make. Cover the tube with paper or fabric. The number of pieces you need will depend on your design. We used three different pieces (head, shirt, pants) for the baseball player and two pieces (head and body) for both the fairy and circus clown.

2 Decorate. Remember to make all designs from the center so the face, shirt buttons, and pants line up properly. We created facial features with colored pencils and black pen. For the baseball player, we made clothes and a baseball glove from colored paper. Our clown is dressed in plaid wrapping paper, rickrack, and yarn. He has yarn hair and paper hands and feet. Our fairy also has yarn hair. She is wearing a felt and netting dress, and has wings and a magic wand made from chenille sticks. Don't forget a star for the wand.

3 Carefully glue the pieces made in Step 2 in place on the tube. We made hats from construction paper. Cut a half-circle of paper—a small one for the baseball cap and a bigger one for the clown. Curve into a cone shape and glue. Don't forget to add a bill to the baseball cap.

More Ideas

Make and give the puppets as party favors, or your guests can make their own. Make several puppets and group them together as a centerpiece.

Tube Tower Puzzle

Three-dimensional puzzles are quite popular. Make one like ours or create some of your own.

You Will Need:

- cardboard tube of any size
- paint, crayons, markers
- scissors

1 Think about a design for your puzzle. We did an easy one, using an abstract design of bright colors. How about making a building, a rocket, or a penguin?

2 Carefully cut your "tower" into three or four pieces. Lightly squeeze the tube to get your cuts started. Jagged or slanted cuts are the easiest. Your cuts need to be exact so the pieces will fit together. If you want to make curvy cuts, ask an adult to help you.

More Ideas

Make puzzles that have interchangeable parts. Making heads, bodies, and legs of people or animals that you could mix and match would be lots of fun.

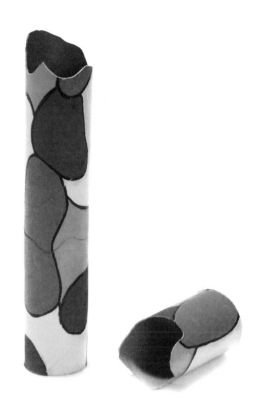

Hanger Wreath

For a holiday or any day, a wreath is a wonderful decoration.

You Will Need:

- cardboard tubes
- wire hanger
- paint
- ribbon
- colored paper
- tissue paper
- scissors
- glue

1 Ask an adult to help you bend the wire hanger into a circle shape.

2 You'll need 10-15 tubes. Make horizontal cuts in the middle of each tube; stop when you are halfway through. Decorate the tubes and then push the slit of each tube onto the hanger.

3 Cut out leaves and glue them between the tubes. Look at our picture for help. Crumple tissue papers and attach. Add a colorful bow at the top.

More Ideas

Change the colors and make a wreath for each season.

›aring Tubes

Let your imagination soar as you create these "high-flying" crafts. Aren't tubes perfect bodies for planes, rockets, and helicopters?

You Will Need:

- cardboard tubes
- lightweight cardboard or foam paper
- paint, crayons, markers
- construction paper
- scissors
- glue or tape
- chenille sticks
- metal fasteners
- decorative items

1 Choose the aircraft you want to make. Then decide how big you want the body to be and get the right-sized tube. We used bathroom tissue and paper towel tubes, but wouldn't a rocket made from a big, sturdy wrapping paper tube be fun?

2 Decorate your tube. If you use paint, use a thick one that covers well. The cardboard that most tubes are made from is hard to cover with paint—the glued sections show through. We used lots of acrylic paint on our helicopter. Choosing a dark color works best. Sometimes it's better to glue white paper to the tube as described in Step 3 and then paint the paper the color you want.

3 You can skip Step 2 and just cover your tube with colorful construction paper. Measure the length or height of your tube and trim your paper to fit. Then lightly wrap the paper around the tube to see about how much paper you need. Cut the paper to the correct size, apply glue, and attach the paper to the tube. Smooth the paper carefully as you wrap it around the tube.

Soar even more as you pretend to pilot these aircraft on wondrous adventures to exciting places. Today you can be giving city traffic reports from a helicopter. Tomorrow, be an astronaut.

To Make the Helicopter

Make the body. Punch four holes in the tube and insert landing gear made from chenille sticks. Next cut a 1" section from another tube and trim away two small arcs from its bottom so it will fit neatly on the tube body. Decorate. Cover the open top with a paper circle and set aside. For the tail section make a long, thin cone. Next make propellers of two different sizes from lightweight cardboard or foam paper and attach with the metal fasteners. Attach the top section to the tube, slide the cone onto the back, and secure with glue or tape. You're ready to whirl away.

To Make the Rocket

Decorate the tube as described in Step 2 on page 12. One way to make the cone is to cut a half-circle out of construction paper, roll one side in, and tape or glue. We made ours about 3" tall. Attach the cone to the top of the tube. Cut out two or four tail fins from lightweight cardboard or foam paper. Use lots of glue to attach the fins to the rocket body securely. Add details with paper cutouts, markers, or other materials. We even used some sequins. It's blast-off time!

To Make the Airplane

Make the basic body. We covered ours with colored construction paper. We made windows with paper cutouts and markers. Make a short cone for the nose of the plane and decorate before attaching. We added a foil point to ours. Cut wings and triangular tail sections from cardboard or foam paper. Attach with lots of glue. Now fly, fly away.

More Ideas

Make several different soaring tubes, attach fishing line, and hang them from the ceiling of your room.

Instead of a passenger jet, make a military plane. Or try your hand at making an old-fashioned prop plane, a modern glider, or an ultralight plane.

Use several tubes and design your own space shuttle or orbiting space station.

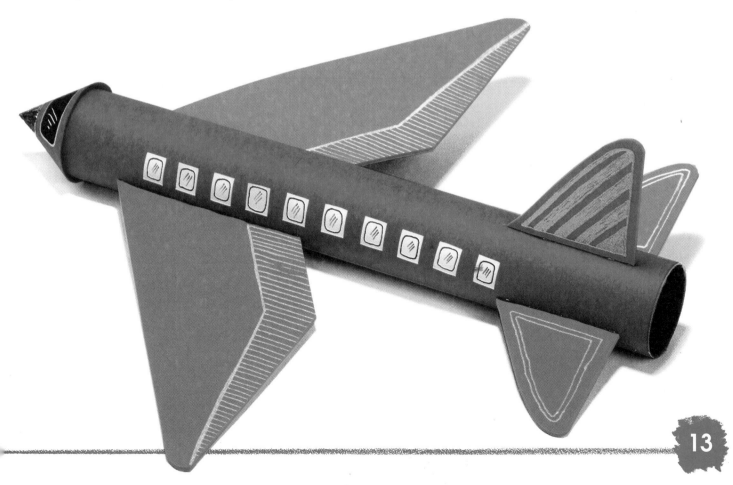

Raft of Tubes

Get away from it all as you pretend to float away downriver.

You Will Need:

- cardboard tubes
- ice-cream sticks
- paint or colored paper
- yarn
- scissors
- glue

1 Decorate your tubes for the raft's bottom. We used six paper towel tubes. Glue on an ice-cream stick floor. We made a railing from pieces of tiny tubes (from fabric softener) and yarn.

2 Attach two tubes to the floor for the roof-support poles. Decorate the roof tubes and begin to cut them in half, stopping before going all the way through. Bend and glue them to each other and then to an ice-cream stick. Glue the stick to the support poles and attach another tube in the bend.

More Ideas

Glue a plastic-foam tray to the bottom and your raft will float.

Make-It Monster

A monster isn't quite so scary when you create it yourself.

You Will Need:

- cardboard tubes
- paint
- scissors
- glue
- various items for decoration

1 Design and sketch your monster. Then cut out pieces of tubes. We used a variety of sizes. Paint the tubes inside and out. We used the naturally curved parts of the tubes to make wings, feet, and a tail. If you want the jagged look, ask an adult to help you cut the tubes.

2 Glue the tubes together, allowing time for the glue to set. Then add facial features. We used chenille sticks, paper circles, and pompons.

More Ideas

Instead of a monster, make a modern art sculpture like you might see at playgrounds.

Roaring Tubes

Make your own trucks, buses, cars, and construction equipment. Don't forget to make the *roaring* sound as you play.

You Will Need:

- cardboard tubes
- lightweight cardboard or foam board
- construction paper or foam paper
- chenille sticks
- plastic-drinking straws
- paint, markers, or colored pencils

1 Choose a vehicle to make. Look at our pictures for help in deciding on the shape. Notice the sleek windshield of the race car. Making the rounded cab of the truck and the bulldozer's curved blade is easy because of the tubes' rounded shape.

2 Cut your tubes and decorate them. We drew windows on our bus and used construction paper and foam paper to cover some of the vehicles' cabs and windshields.

3 Make holes where the wheels will go on your vehicle. Use a hole punch if it will reach. Otherwise, ask an adult to help you. Also make holes so the van and trailer can be attached. We used a chenille stick, but yarn will work, too.

4 Put a plastic-drinking straw through the holes you made in the body of your vehicle so that the straw is inside, like an axle. Or, simply glue the straw to the bottom of the vehicle where you want the wheels to go. If you do this, you can skip Step 3.

5 Cut out wheels and punch a hole in the center of each one. Cut pieces of chenille stick that are at least ½" longer than the straw pieces. Push a chenille stick through the straw, and thread the wheels on its ends. Twist and you're ready to roll.

More Ideas

Make an engine and train cars. String them together with yarn. Or make and give these vehicles as stocking stuffers.

Have a transportation-themed birthday party. Surround the cake with a variety of these vehicles. Give a roaring tube to each guest as a party favor. Or even better, let guests make their own.

Musical Tubes

Sing a song, dance a jig, play a tune, keep the beat—all fun ways to enjoy these musical crafts. Isn't it amazing how many instruments are shaped like cardboard tubes?

You Will Need:

- cardboard tubes
- paint or colored paper
- scissors
- glue
- waxed paper
- rubber bands
- paper cup
- aluminum foil
- metal fasteners
- dried beans or popcorn kernels
- various items for decoration: yarn, foam paper, rickrack, ribbon

To Make the Basic Instrument

Choose the instrument you want to make and read the directions. Each one calls for some different materials, so you won't need all the items included in the list. Decorate your tube with paint or cover it with some colorful paper of any type—wrapping, construction, even tissue paper.

To Make the Bass Bog

We used a 7" section of tube. (That is a good size for an average rubber band to stretch around.) Then we covered the tube with paper that we had already painted with watercolors. Make two small cuts on opposite sides of one end of the tube. Do the same on the other end, keeping those cuts in line with the first cuts. Stretch a large rubber band and place it in the cuts. Pluck the rubber band at one of the open ends. Does it sound like a frog?

To Make the Rhythm Tube

Decorate your tube. Put a little glue around one of its ends and cover that end with layers of aluminum foil, carefully placing the edges of the foil on top of the glue. Let it dry. Pour beans or popcorn kernels into the open end of the tube. Then glue a piece of foil to that end. Add yarn circles, tassels, or other decorations, and you're ready to keep the beat for the neighborhood band.

Invite some friends, have an instrument-making party, and then strike up the band. Perform for your families—just pick some favorite songs that you all know.

To Make the Clarinet

Choose a tube and decorate it. Maybe you'll want to make yours look more like a real clarinet than we did. Ours is short and colorful. Ask an adult to help you use a large nail or pointed scissors to make four or five holes that are about ¼" across. Put them about 1" apart. Cut off the bottom of a small paper cup and discard it. The rest of the cup will be the "bell" of the clarinet. First decorate the cup and then glue or tape it to one end of the tube. Cover the opening of the bell with waxed paper. We used a rubber band to hold it in place. Move your fingers over the holes while you hum a tune into the open end.

To Make the Rain Stick

Decorate your tube. We put patches of brightly colored paint directly on a paper towel tube. Ask an adult to help you use a very small nail to poke holes in the tube. Put a tiny drop of glue around each hole and insert a metal paper fastener in each one. Cover one end of the tube with aluminum foil and glue it in place. Pour in large dried beans and cover the other end with foil and decorate. Gently turn the tube on end and listen to the sound of rain as the beans fall against the metal fasteners. Instruments like these were used by native peoples of Central and South America to invoke rain.

To Make the Kazoo

Nothing could be easier than making a kazoo, so why not make lots of them—they're great party favors! Decorate your tube. A bathroom tissue tube is just the right size, or cut the length you want from a longer tube. We covered our tube with colorful plaid wrapping paper. Attach a piece of waxed paper to one end of the tube. Use glue or hold it in place with a rubber band. We put a decorative piece of foam paper around each end of ours. Hum a tune into the open end of the tube.

More Ideas

Use the basic clarinet directions and make a recorder. Make a "mouthpiece" by squeezing the tube at the open end. Make holes of different sizes in this order from the mouthpiece: one medium, two large, one medium, one large, and two sets of two small ones side-by-side. Remember that the bell of a recorder is smaller than a clarinet's. Can you figure out how to make a flute?

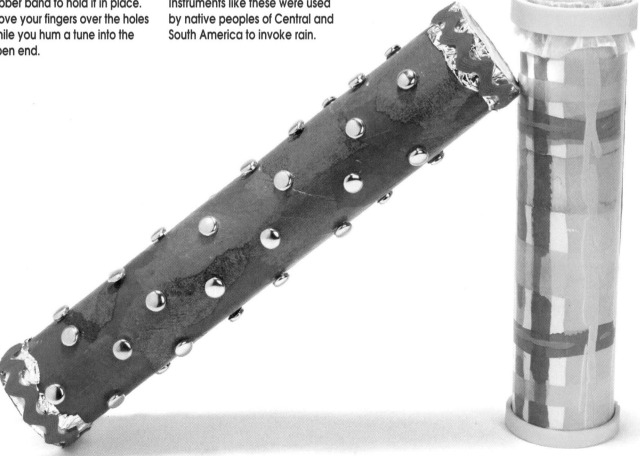

Menorah

Candles are an important part of celebrations. You see them for all seasons and special occasions. Using a cardboard tube is an easy way for you to begin your own candle making.

1 Cut two rectangular pieces of cardboard. (We cut up a gift box.) Our base is 11" long and 5" wide. The upper candle-holder part is 15" long and 3" wide. Paint both and let dry.

2 Paint your cardboard tubes or cover them with colored paper. We used a total of seven bathroom tissue tubes. We cut four of the tubes in half to make eight shorter tubes.

3 Decorate the "posts" by wrapping ribbon around two of the tubes. Attach the candle-holder part and base cardboard to these tubes. The tubes go between the two pieces of cardboard as shown. Use lots of glue around the rims of the tubes and position them carefully. Hold in place until the glue is set.

4 Cut out nine sets of 5" squares of red, orange, and yellow tissue paper. Overlap and twist each set to form a flame shape. Glue to the inside of the nine candle tubes.

5 Glue the one remaining tall tube, called the Shamos, in the exact middle of the candle-holder cardboard. Glue it securely and then glue the short candles in place as shown.

More Ideas

Celebrate Christmas with an Advent candle ring. Use a sturdy paper plate as a base. Make one pink and three purple candles, gluing them in a circle shape. Depending on your faith, you may want to make a red or white center candle.

Celebrate Kwanzaa with a kinara. Make cardboard base and candle-holder parts like the menorah's. There are seven kinara candles. To depict the order of lighting and the relative amount of time the candles have "burned," you can make them differ in length. For example, if the longest is 4 ½" tall, the next one will be 4", the next 3 ½", and so on, with the shortest being 1 ½". Glue them on the cardboard in order from longest to shortest, left to right. The three tallest candles should be red, the middle one black, and the others green.

Talking Tubes

Communicate like the children of long ago.

You Will Need:

- cardboard tubes
- waxed paper
- rubber bands
- 10'-20' of heavy thread or dental floss
- paper clips
- paint or construction paper
- scissors
- glue or tape

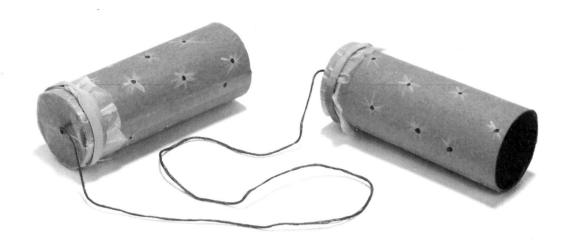

1 Decorate two tubes. Cut two circles of waxed paper and poke a tiny hole in the center of each. Insert one end of the thread through each hole. Tie a paper clip to the end of the thread.

2 Put the paper clip inside the tube and secure the waxed paper to the tube with a rubber band. Give a friend one tube and you keep the other. Go far enough apart so that the string is tight and start talking!

More Ideas

Create a mystery play where you'll need to use your talking tubes. For even more fun, make up a secret code.

Napkin Rings

Brighten your table with these easy-to-make crafts.

You Will Need:

- cardboard tubes
- scissors
- glue
- tape
- various items for decoration

1 Cut 1" to 2" sections from tubes. Paper towel or bathroom tissue tubes are just the right size.

2 Decorate your sections. We wound yarn around one, ribbon around another, and covered one with paper with ribbon borders. Choosing holiday colors or colors that match your dishes would be nice.

More Ideas

Attach paper cutouts to the top of your napkin rings. Try flowers, bunnies, autumn leaves, or circles with each guest's name.

Games Galore

We all know that playing games can be a lot of fun. Now you'll see that making the games can be great fun, too. We'll give you directions for making a few games. You'll probably think of others to make.

You Will Need:

- cardboard tubes
- plastic-foam trays
- cardboard or foam board
- colored paper
- scissors
- glue
- paint, crayons, markers
- plastic rings
- clothespins
- uncooked macaroni
- foam ball
- die

1 Choose the game or games you want to make. Think about the materials you will need. You will probably need lots of tubes, so your first step may be to start saving tubes several weeks ahead of time. Or contact your neighbors and friends and ask them to start saving tubes. It's amazing how fast tubes will accumulate when lots of folks are saving them.

2 Look at the pictures of the game or games you want to make so you can get the correct number and size of tubes. Asking an adult to help will make the cutting easier and safer. Paint or cover the tubes with construction paper. Letting your imagination run wild as you decorate can be fun, too. Our tubes are plain but colorful.

To Make the Ring Toss

Decorate a large plastic-foam tray. Ours is 9" x 12". Be sure to have at least two different colored sections. Ours are white and deep pink. Put a number, such as 10, on your decorated tube and glue the tube to the tray. Put numbers in the other sections. Looking at our picture will help. Get two rings that are 2"-3" across. We made ours by cutting out the insides of plastic lids. Ask an adult to help you or use an old bangle bracelet. Or make cardboard rings from large wrapping paper tubes. You're ready to toss the rings and keep score. With our board, we give 10 points for ringers, 5 points if the ring is mostly in the white area, and 2 points for the dark pink. Rings that fall totally on the floor don't get any points.

Why not have an Olympics party? Set up lots of different games like these for your friends to try—remember to reward effort and improvement, too.

To Make the Clothespin Game

Paint a plastic-foam tray, a piece of cardboard, or a piece of foam board. We used a 5" x 9" piece of foam board. Glue your decorated tube to the center of the board. Don't you like our polka-dotted, ribbon-based one? Grab a friend and some clothespins—it's game time. See how many times each of you can get a clothespin into the tube out of ten tries. To make the game more challenging, try dropping the clothespins faster and faster and/or by raising your arm higher and higher.

To Make the Macaroni Marathon

Decorate a piece of cardboard or foam board. We painted a 7" x 20" piece of foam board, but the bottom of a large cardboard box will work just as well. Cut out sixteen pieces of tube that are each about 1 ½" high. Decorate them as two different sets. Cut out four pieces of tube about 3" high. Decorate two to match each set of your short tubes. Put START and FINISH on each pair. Attach the tubes to your board as shown in the picture. Play as a toss game for two players, seeing how many tosses it takes to get from START to FINISH or see *More Ideas* for directions on how to play it as a relay game.

To Make the Bowling Pins

Choose at least three different sizes of tubes. We made six pins, but you could make ten, like in a bowling alley. Decorate your pins. Make them colorful like ours that are covered with construction paper. Or paint them to look more "real." Set the pins up and try to knock them down with a foam or yarn ball. Keep score as though you were really bowling.

More Ideas

To play Macaroni Marathon as a relay, each player puts ten pieces of macaroni in the START cups. Take turns rolling a die and moving your pieces up your side. The first player to reach the FINISH cup with all pieces wins. Hint: You can break up a roll—for example, if you roll a six, you can move one piece up by four cups and a different piece up by two.

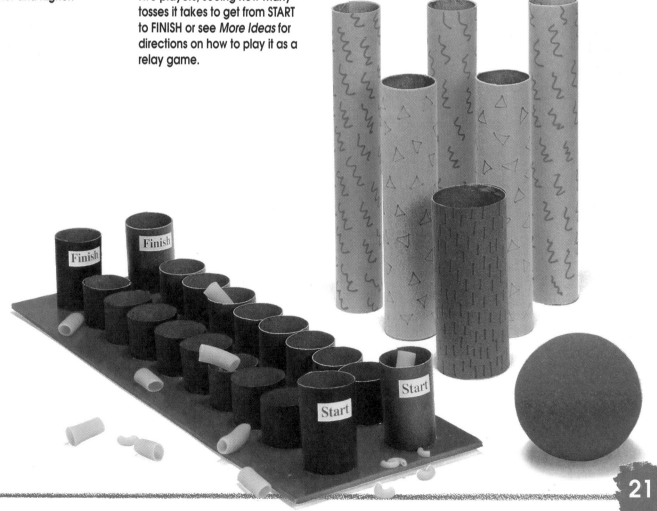

Desk Organizer

Make your own holder to keep supplies handy and neat.

You Will Need:

- cardboard tubes
- colored paper
- paint
- plastic-foam tray
- scissors
- glue
- various items for decoration

1 Design your organizer. Choose a variety of tubes and cut sections of differing heights. Decorate with paint and/or colored paper. We painted our tubes and trimmed them with wavy strips of painted paper.

2 Paint the tray and let dry. Then decorate the tray. Finally, glue the tubes to the tray. Hold them in place until the glue sets.

More Ideas

Instead of a plastic-foam tray, use a shoe box lid or trim the bottom 2" from a tissue box. Add MOM or DAD letters for a "special day" gift.

"Write" Props

Decorate or play with these oversized and kooky crafts.

You Will Need:

- cardboard tubes
- construction paper
- colored pencils, paint, or markers
- scissors
- glue or tape

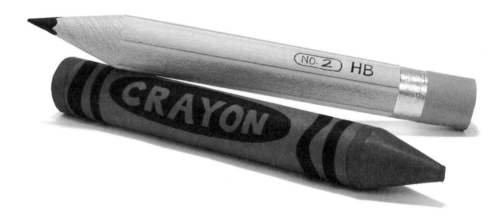

To Make the Pencil

Make and decorate a cone for the pencil's point. Ours is about 3" long and made from paper that we decorated with marker and colored pencils. Paint or cover a large tube to look like a pencil. Don't forget the eraser. Insert the wide part of the cone into the other end of the tube and glue or tape.

To Make the Crayon

Choose a color for your crayon. Form a cone for the point from a 2" x 5" rectangle of decorated paper. Cover the opening with a small circle of paper. Decorate the tube. Looking at a real crayon will help with the details. Insert the cone into the tube and secure it with glue or tape. Glue a paper circle over the open end.

More Ideas

To help a preschooler learn colors, make a set of crayons in basic colors.

Make the eraser part of the pencil from a paper cup or piece of tube that is slightly larger than the pencil. Slide the eraser off and store pencils or other surprises inside the tube.

Tube Tea Set

It's fun to dress up and pretend to serve tea to your friends. And it's just as much fun to make a tea set of your own design.

You Will Need:

- cardboard tubes
- paint
- colored paper
- plastic-foam tray
- scissors
- glue
- various items for decoration: buttons, beads, rickrack, stickers, glitter, chenille sticks

1 Cut a section from a large wrapping paper tube for the teapot. Ours is 4" tall. Cut sections from a medium-sized tube for your cups. We used smaller tubes for our cream and sugar containers, but you can use whatever size you choose.

2 Decorate your tubes. We sponge painted ours, but covering them with wrapping paper or fabric would look terrific. How about an old-fashioned flowered design? (Don't forget to paint the insides of the tubes, too.)

3 To make the spouts, first cut triangular shapes from the tubes. It's easiest to start at the edge, like our creamer. Ask an adult to help if you start below the edge, like our teapot. The spouts are made from pieces of colored paper folded and glued inside the tubes.

4 Make handles from strips of colored paper or lightweight cardboard. Chenille sticks would work well, too. Just form a curve and glue the two ends to the container.

5 Make cone-shaped lids from sheets of half-circle paper. Glue on a button or bead knob. Put the set on a decorated plastic-foam tray, and you're ready to say, "Tea is served."

More Ideas

Make a complete set of pretend dinnerware. Decorate large and small paper plates and soup bowls to match your tea set.

More Games Galore

You probably never realized how many games involve tube-shaped elements. Here are a few more that are easy to make. Collecting the tubes could be the hardest part.

You Will Need:

- cardboard tubes
- cardboard or foam board
- construction paper
- small paper cup
- paint, crayons, markers
- scissors
- glue
- yarn
- large button
- small buttons or coins
- marbles

1 Look at the games pictured here. Decide which one you want to make. Maybe you'll decide to make them all. Just be sure you have enough tubes—plan ahead and start saving early.

2 Decorate your tubes with paint or cover them with construction paper. If you use paint, remember that some cardboard tubes really soak up paint, so you have to use a lot and give it time to dry. That's true for all the crafts in this book. If you cover them with paper, you'll find that it's smart to measure and trim your paper before you start to glue or tape it to the tube.

To Make the Tunnel Game

Decorate five or more tubes. Cut out a ½"-¾" strip from the length of the tube. Looking at our picture will help. Paint the insides of the tubes and then glue them together with the open side down. That's all you really have to do for this game except assign a point value to each tunnel. We made ours fancier by painting and then attaching a foam-board top. Then we used more foam board to make a wavy backdrop to display the point values. Cardboard will work, too. Get your marbles, and try to roll them into the tunnels. How high can you score with ten tries?

Not only are games fun to play and to make, they are great gifts. Everyone really likes to get something that you've made yourself.

To Make the Coin Game

Cut and decorate a large piece of cardboard or foam board. Ours is 8" x 14" and painted bright gold. Decorate ten bathroom tissue tubes. We covered ours with construction paper, and used sticker-type numbers to show the point value of each tube. Writing numbers on with a marker or crayon will work just as well. Glue the tubes to the base. Be sure all your numbers face the same way. We placed our tubes with the high point values in the middle and the lower ones near the edges of the board. You're ready to get a friend and take turns trying to toss a coin into one of the tubes—the higher its point value, the better. Don't stand directly over the board. As you become good at the game, stand farther and farther away.

To Make the Thread-the-Tube Game

Decorate a bathroom tissue tube anyway you like. We painted ours green and then glued on stripes of yellow construction paper. Punch a hole near one end of the tube. Get a piece of yarn or ribbon that is 12"-18" long. Tie one end through the hole in the tube and the other to a large button. To play, hold the tube in an upright position as shown in the picture. Swing the button in an upward motion, trying to get it to go into the tube. We think making the game is much easier than playing it!

To Make the Button-Toss Game

Decorate a bathroom tissue tube and attach a small paper cup to one end. We painted both pieces red. Decorate a piece of cardboard, foam board, or a plastic-foam tray. Create sections like those in our picture. We drew two ovals about 2" apart. That left four corner areas. Then we assigned a point value to each area. Glue the tube in the center of the base and assign it a point value. Step back and try to toss your buttons into the cup. Play by yourself or with a friend. How many points can you get with five buttons?

More Ideas

Instead of tossing buttons in the Button Toss Game, put the game board on a table and try to flip or flick the buttons up and into the cup.

Can you figure out how to use four tubes and a cardboard base to make a football goalpost? Use a button or small ball as your football and try to "kick it" through the goalpost with your thumb and index fingers. To make the game even more challenging, keep moving your "football" farther away.

Story-Time Mobiles

All mobiles are fascinating to watch. And they can be just as fascinating and fun to make. These are really special—you can use them as puppets, too. Preschoolers will really like watching them.

You Will Need:

- cardboard tubes
- ice-cream sticks
- yarn or ribbon
- paint, crayons, markers
- construction paper
- lightweight cardboard or foam paper
- scissors
- glue
- various items for decoration: plastic-foam ball, plastic eyes, tissue paper, chenille sticks

1 Choose a tube that is no smaller than a paper towel tube. We used 24" wrapping paper tubes. Choose a theme and decorate your tube with paint or construction paper. We painted our tube first and then added other decorations.

For the Ocean Theme

We made an octopus from a plastic-foam ball with foam-paper tentacles. Our crab is painted cardboard and chenille sticks. Our cute clam is a simple circle colored and folded in half with eyes peeking out.

2 Ask an adult to help you make holes in the tube. The first one should be about 3" from the end. Make another hole directly beneath it. Make two more pairs of holes—one set in the center and the other set 3" from the opposite end of the tube.

For the Space Theme

We made a silver foam-board spaceship with tissue paper exhaust and used foam paper for our three-eyed friendly green alien and crescent-moon man.

3 Make three 12"-15" pieces of yarn and tie each to the center of an ice-cream stick. Thread the other yarn end through a pair of the holes in the tube. Pull down until the stick rests on the top of the tube. Tie a hanging object to the end of each piece of yarn.

More Ideas

Make up a story about your mobile. Then act it out. Of course, you know you can make a mobile with any theme you want!

Ribbon Holder

This "hound" will keep your ribbon where you need it.

You Will Need:

- cardboard tube
- sturdy cardboard or foam board
- scissors
- glue
- various items for decoration

1 Decorate a section of tube for the dog's body. Cut out the dog's front and back from cardboard or foam board, decorate, and attach to the tube with glue.

2 We made our tail section removable so ribbon holders can slide on. Just cut a 2" section of tube, cut out a tiny slice, and tape the edges of the cut back together. This makes it slightly smaller than the dog's body so it will slip inside it easily.

More Ideas

How about a holder that looks like a dinosaur or a centipede?

Sitting Scarecrow

Make a friend for your indoor garden, mantel, or table.

You Will Need:

- cardboard tube
- fabric or paper
- paint or markers
- yarn
- scissors
- glue

1 Choose a tube for the head and body. Ours is 7" long. Decorate and add facial features. We used a checked fabric for the shirt and brown paper for the head.

2 Create arms and legs from fabric or paper. Ribbon will work, too. We used burlap. We covered the lower part of the tube, too. Glue to the bottom and back of the tube.

3 Add hands, feet, and hair. We used yarn and added a burlap hat.

More Ideas

Use red felt and make a sitting Santa or green for St. Patrick's Day leprechauns.

A Crowd of Creatures

Creatures, creatures everywhere and all such fun to make! Make "real" ones or imaginary friend ones—just put on your creative thinking cap.

You Will Need:

- cardboard tubes
- cardboard or foam board
- paint, crayons, markers
- construction paper
- various items for decoration: moveable plastic eyes, chenille sticks
- stapler
- scissors
- glue

1 Choose a creature to make. Create one of these or imagine one of your own to test your crafting skills. Get a tube that suits the size you want your creature to be. How about working with a really large wrapping paper tube to create a giant creature for your room? Just don't get carried away and get your room too crowded.

2 You may want to trim the ends of your tube to give your creature a distinctive head and tail. You'll be surprised at how easy it is and what a difference it makes. See how the mouths of our lobster, fish, and dinosaur differ. Look at their tails, too. We'll tell you how we did it in the directions that follow.

To Make the Lobster

Cut a 1 ½" wedge from one end of a paper towel tube. Then make a place for the claws by cutting a 1" slit on each side. You can see in our picture exactly where to put the slits. You can also see how to cut the shape of the lobster's tail. Ask an adult to help you make three holes in each side of the tube and two more holes for its eyes. Paint or cover the tube with construction paper. Make a tail and claws from construction paper. Insert and glue the claws in the slits. Then insert the tail, squeeze the end of the tube, and staple. Insert chenille-stick legs and "eyes." Add beads and your lobster is ready for fun.

Isn't it great to give each creature an expression that reveals its personality? We think our fish is happy and our porcupine puzzled. Do you agree?

To Make the Fish

Choose a tube and decorate it. We painted a bathroom-tissue-sized one. A couple of simple cuts will create a mouth for your fish. Ask an adult to help you make a 2" slit in the fish's back. Create a tail and fins—ours were made with colored pencils on blue construction paper cut into wavy shapes. Glue on the side fins. Push the top fin into the fish's mouth and pull it up through the slit. Insert the tail fin, squeeze the back of the tube, and staple. Add moveable plastic eyes and display your fish.

To Make the Porcupine

Choose a tube and decorate it. We painted a bathroom tissue tube gray. To make the quills, we cut out six 4" x 5" rectangles. Then we cut out triangular sections about 3 ½" tall to make the spikes. This leaves a ½" tab at the bottom. Wrap each strip around the tube and glue it on. Fold up the spikes. Add cardboard or foam-board legs and a paper tail. Make a head of your own design or like ours, which is construction paper with moveable plastic eyes and marker-made ears, nose, and mouth. Your porcupine is ready to roam.

To Make the Dinosaur

Our dinosaur is made from a 10" section of a sturdy wrapping paper tube. We covered it in green speckle-painted paper. V-cuts were made for the mouth and a slant cut for the tail. Ask an adult to help you cut if your tube is real thick. Our foam-board legs are covered with the same paper as the body. Then we added back plates and a tongue made from construction paper. Marker-made eyes complete our creature.

More Ideas

Crocodiles, caterpillars, and centipedes would be natural additions to your crowd of creatures. Can you figure out how to make an octopus from a ball and eight tubes?

Write a story about your creature. If you make the whole crowd, try to write one story that involves them all.

Make a school of different kinds of fish. Find pictures of real fish and try to make lifelike models. Wouldn't that be a great science project?

Tube Turkey

Here's the perfect Thanksgiving table decoration.

1 Our turkey's tail is seven brightly painted paper towel tubes. His body is a 6" section of a large wrapping paper tube. The head, chest, feet, wattle, and beak are construction-paper cutouts.

2 Mount the body on a piece of cardboard to keep it steady. Ask an adult to help you make a 1 ½" slit for the tail. Squeeze the bottoms of the long tubes, hold them together like a fan, and staple. Insert the "tail" in the slit you made and glue. The feathers are the finishing touch.

More Ideas

Make a bright peacock.

Flags for All Seasons

People love to decorate with flags.

1 Paint or cover a long tube with paper.

2 Cut out a fabric or felt rectangle. Our spring flag is a 9" x 12" piece of felt. The flower is made from pieces of felt and pompons glued to the rectangle. Make three holes along one side and attach to the tube with yarn or chenille sticks.

More Ideas

Covering the pole with plastic or aluminum foil and making the flag from an old shower curtain will make it more waterproof so that you can hang it outdoors.

A Host of Handles

You can make lots of things with handles from cardboard tubes. *Lots of* handles—that's what we mean by a *host of* handles.

You Will Need:

- cardboard tubes
- construction paper
- lightweight cardboard
- paint, crayons, markers
- scissors
- glue or tape

More Ideas

Wouldn't these crafts make great props for a play? Or you could use them in an advertising display for a playground clean-up day.

Make pretend housecleaning tools. For a broom, you could insert a bundle of straw. A bundle of yarn would make a great head for a mop.

Make sports equipment. A golf club or hockey stick will be easy. Can you figure out how to create a lacrosse stick or rackets for tennis or badminton?

1 Get a long cardboard wrapping paper tube for each tube tool you want to make. Or, you can make a long tube from two or three paper towel tubes. Just tape or glue the tubes together. If you use glue, it will help to squeeze one tube as you insert it into the other.

To Make the Hoe

Use a tube with at least a 4" diameter. You can also use an oatmeal box to give you a curve like the hoe we made. Cut out a section shaped like the one in our picture. It is about 7" long with a 5" curve with a tab cut to fit up into the handle. Paint and attach to the inside of the handle with glue or tape.

To Make the Shovel

From lightweight cardboard, cut out a shovel-shape as shown. (Don't forget to include a long tab.) Paint it. Shading its center with pencil will make it look more realistic. Attach to inside of the handle.

2 You can leave the tube handles their natural brown color, paint them like we did, or cover them with colored paper.

To Make the Rake

Use a wrapping paper tube with about a 2" diameter. Cut out a section like ours, about 10" long with a tab at the top. Paint it. Ask an adult to help cut out the tines—the forklike sections of the rake. Insert the tab into the handle and attach it securely with tape or glue.

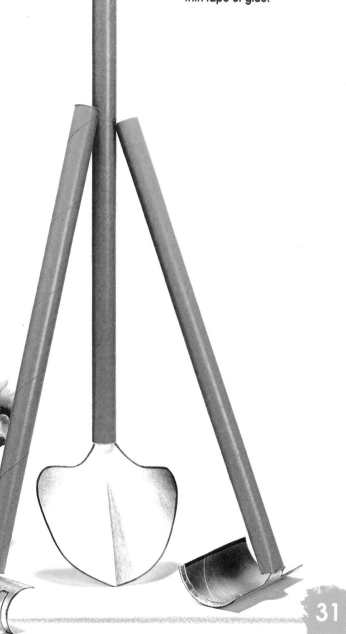

Ye Olde Tube Town

Hear ye, hear ye! This jolly play town is easy to make—and even more fun to play with. Fire up your imagination, get or make some medieval action figures, and begin a grand adventure.

You Will Need:

- cardboard tubes
- scissors
- construction paper
- glue
- tape
- paint, crayons, markers

1 Gather lots of cardboard tubes—short ones, tall ones, skinny ones, fat ones. Make a plan for the buildings you want to create for your town. Making a rough sketch will help. Ask an adult to help you cut the tubes to the various lengths needed for your plan.

2 Think about what you want your village to look like. Choose your colors and get a supply of paint, markers, crayons, and/or construction paper or paper that you can decorate yourself.

3 Decorate your tubes. We painted ours "building" colors: brown, rust, tan, and gray. (Remember paint needs time to dry.) Then we used markers and paint to create windows and doors. We even added some grass and shrubs around the bottom. It's easy to draw or paint stones, but for a more realistic look, glue on some small rocks and pebbles.

Wouldn't this be a great stage backdrop for a puppet play performed by you and your friends? Invite all your parents and serve old English tea and peasant black bread.

4 Create roofs for your buildings. We used cones made from construction paper. (One way to make a cone is to start with a paper or lightweight cardboard circle, cut out a wedge like a slice of pie, and then tape or glue the edges together.) We also made thatched roofs from construction paper decorated with markers and colored pencils. (You could also glue dried grass or hay to a piece of cardboard.) Start with a rectangle with wavy edges, fold it in half, and then fold one edge under to form a tab. Glue the tab to the top of the building.

5 Arrange the tubes to make the building you sketched in Step 1. Don't put the tubes in a straight row. Stagger them in and out, placing some behind others. You can vary the placement of the towers on your buildings as we did, too. Just make two cuts in the bottom of a short tube and slide it over the front side of another taller tube. Finally, glue the tubes together to form several different groups of buildings .

More Ideas

Create other parts for your town. Can you figure out how to make trees, bridges, and fences from cardboard tubes?

Use the ideas for finger puppets on page 10 to create some medieval characters for your town. Remember to "size" the puppets according to how big your buildings are.

Make a moat for one of your castles. Cut a paper towel tube in half lengthwise, place it so it looks like a ditch, and paint in "water." Make a drawbridge from lightweight cardboard and yarn or chenille sticks.

If modern cities are more to your liking, decorate the tubes to look like high-rise skyscrapers. For a futuristic look, wrap the tubes in foil or paint them with wild colors of metallic paints.

Lions, Tigers, and Bears

Oh my! These beasts are more friendly than fierce. Wouldn't they look great decorating a baby's or toddler's room? Just put them out of reach of little hands.

You Will Need:

- cardboard tubes
- cardboard
- scissors
- glue
- construction paper
- chenille sticks
- plastic lids
- paint, crayons, markers
- various items for decoration: plastic eyes, fuzzy pompons, felt, fabric, and fake fur scraps

1 For legs, cut four tubes of equal length. Ours are 3" to 4" long. Decorate the legs. Cover them with paper or fabric, or paint them and set aside to dry.

3 To make the head, use paper, cardboard, or plastic lids. Here's what we did: For the lion, we cut a construction-paper circle, fringed the edges, and drew in lines to make it look like a mane. For the tiger, we glued a construction-paper circle onto a plastic lid, and we covered a plastic lid with furlike fabric for the bear. Then we added facial features, using plastic eyes, pompons, construction paper, marker, and chenille sticks.

2 Cut a cardboard square for the body. We made ours about 4" x 4", but you can make one as large or small as you like. Decorate the body to match your animal's legs.

4 Assemble your animal. First glue the legs to the body, and let the glue set. All four of our legs touch. If you're making a bigger animal, attach the legs to the four corners of the body. Glue on the head.

5 Make tails and attach. We twisted chenille sticks together for the tiger, attached a small fur square to the bear, and partially covered chenille sticks with felt for the lion.

More Ideas

Make a whole zoo! Use the basic body instructions to make rhinos, zebras, and elephants. Longer legs and a paper-tube neck make a stately giraffe. Let your imagination run "wild!"

Find some tiny tubes like those from fabric softener rolls, make little animals, and turn the raft on page 14 into Noah's Ark.

Candle Canister

What a lovely way to present a gift of candles or to store your own!

You Will Need:

- cardboard tube
- paint or paper
- scissors
- glue
- ribbon or other decorative items
- 2 small paper cups

1 Choose a tube—a section of a wrapping paper one will work best. Cut three sections from the tube. Our bottom is 8" and the top is 4". The third section, about 1 ½", is needed to slide the top on, so cut a slit, squeeze slightly, insert it into the bottom section, and attach with glue.

2 Decorate your tube with paint or cover it with paper. We sponge-painted ours and added a ribbon bow. Cut the bottoms off two small paper cups. Then close off the open ends of the canister by inserting the cup bottoms and gluing them in place.

More Ideas

Use the canister to store fireplace matches or knitting needles.

Decorate a canister with your school colors and keep your pens and pencils handy and neat in your bookbag.

Give a painted canister to an artist friend to store brushes in.

Christmas Crackers

Guests twist and pull these traditional holiday favors and goodies pop out.

You Will Need:

- cardboard tube
- wrapping paper
- string, yarn, or ribbon
- various items for decoration

1 Cut the tube in half and place the two pieces back together. Use a tiny piece of tape to hold them in place while you wrap the tube with paper. Be sure your paper is at least 3"-4" longer than your tube.

2 Twist the paper at one end and tie. Pour in small candies and/or prizes through the open end of the tube. Twist the paper and tie. Decorate with ribbon, stickers, garland, or glitter.

More Ideas

In craft stores you'll find an insert that makes the crackers open with a "bang." Or, make a unique package for a present. Leave the tube whole and wrap it. Don't pull it apart; just unwrap!

Mighty Marionettes

Tubes seem to be perfect for making the moveable sections of marionettes. Aren't ours cute? Have a marrionette-making party. Your creations will be cute, too!

You Will Need:

- cardboard tubes
- paint, crayons, markers
- construction paper
- lightweight cardboard or foam paper
- ice-cream sticks
- yarn
- thread, twine, or ribbon
- scissors
- glue

1 Choose the marionette you want to make. If you don't do one of ours, sketch out your plan. It's almost impossible to figure out all the parts and pieces without something to look at as you go along. It's best to decide now how long your strings will need to be. Gather all your materials and get them organized before you begin.

2 For the marionette guide bar, cover a cardboard tube with paper or paint it. Attach two ice-cream sticks as shown in the picture. Use lots of glue. Tie lengths of thread to each end of the stick, wrapping the thread around the stick a few times. Adding a drop of glue will help. The length of the strings is critical to the success of your project, so measure and cut carefully. When you hold the guide bar, the leg strings need to fall straight. If you're new at this, shorter strings are a little easier to work with.

3 Cut sections of cardboard tubes to suit the size of your creature's body, head, tail, and feet. (We'll tell you more about our alligator and giraffe later.) Decorate your tubes. Make tiny holes in the tube where you want to attach the guide thread. Use larger holes for where you'll use yarn to connect the neck and legs to the body.

Creating a marionette is quite a fun-filled challenge, but making it perform can be the most fun of all. Can you "do" the alligator walk? How about making the giraffe nibble from a tree?

4 Insert the guide thread. Dipping the end of the thread (and yarn, too) in glue will make it stiff and easier to get through the holes. Make a big knot or tie a button on the end to hold the thread in place inside the tube. Next pull the yarn through the creature's parts and tie, but don't make it too tight. The head and body need to be able to bend.

To Make the Alligator

Use a 9" section of tube for the body, a 3" head with a mouth cut out, and a 4" squeezed-together tail section. Make feet from four 1" sections of tube. Insert your marionette strings as described above. We used foam-paper circles with holes in the middle to cover the "feet." Then we connected the head, body, tail, and feet with yarn. Don't forget eyes and teeth.

To Make the Giraffe

The body is a 5" section of a wrapping paper tube. The head is a smaller tube about 3 ½" long with a slanted section cut out in the nose area. The feet are 1" tube sections. Our giraffe has a black nose and sleepy eyes. Attach the marionette threads carefully and look at the picture to see how to connect the giraffe's parts with yarn. Don't forget the foam-paper circles, ears, or the yarn tail!

More Ideas

There is no limit to the creatures you can imagine and make.

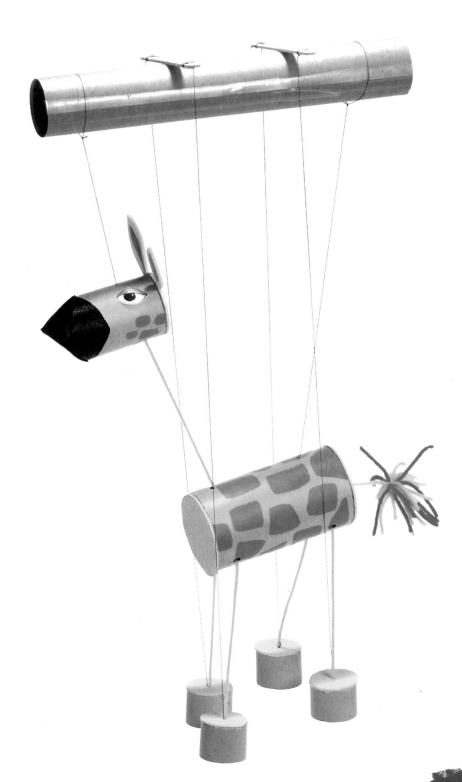

"Bird Feeder" Tube

Use this simple craft as a decoration or hang in a protected area of a porch.

1 Decorate a bathroom tissue tube, or use a section from a wrapping paper tube. We covered ours with sponge-painted paper. Cut a door and punch holes near the tube's bottom. Insert a straw or dowel.

2 Glue a plastic lid to the bottom. Punch holes and insert a chenille stick hanger in the bottom section of a paper cup. Cover the top of the tube with the cup as shown.

More Ideas

To make the feeder more waterproof, cover the tube with plastic wrap or aluminum foil.

Put a fake bird on the straw for an even prettier decoration.

You Will Need:

- cardboard tube
- paper or plastic cup
- plastic lid
- plastic-drinking straw or dowel
- yarn or chenille stick
- glue
- scissors

Tube Binoculars

Set out on a pretend safari or bird-watching expedition with your own "binoculars."

You Will Need:

- cardboard tubes
- paint or paper
- bottle cap
- yarn or ribbon
- construction paper or foam paper
- scissors
- glue

1 Paint two bathroom tissue tubes or cover them with colored paper. We used thick gray paint and then trimmed the tubes with black eye circles and yellow strips of paper.

2 Glue the tubes together. Use a paper clip to hold in place until the glue sets. Glue on the bottle cap as shown. Punch holes at the sides and add a yarn or ribbon strap.

More Ideas

Make your own pretend telescope from tubes of different sizes. Can you mount it on a wrapping-paper-tube tripod?

A Fantastic Fort

Build a big, full-sized fort for you and your friends. Or, build a smaller one for your action figures or dolls. Isn't it fun to pretend to be part of the Old West?

You Will Need:

- cardboard tubes
- heavy cardboard or foam board
- paint, crayons, markers
- large ice-cream stick
- chenille sticks
- scissors

1 Plan to make this craft after the holiday season because you will need as many wrapping paper tubes as you can find, especially if you plan to make a person-sized fort. Remember to ask others to save tubes for you. We used more than three dozen tubes. It's not necessary for all the tubes to be the same.

2 Think about how you want your fort to look. Having a plan will help as you start to glue the tubes together lengthwise. You'll notice we didn't decorate our tubes, but you can paint yours or cover them with paper.

3 Make one wall of your fort at a time. Punch holes in the end tube of each wall. Put them near the top and near the bottom so you can join the walls with twisted chenille sticks. This will allow you to take your fort apart for storage. If you are making a small fort, you can glue the walls together at the corners.

4 Make gates from two pieces of cardboard decorated with paint or markers. Make a latch with chenille sticks and a large ice-cream stick.

5 Make a play ladder from two cardboard tubes and ice-cream sticks. It's really easy. Use it inside or outside the fort.

More Ideas

Make forts for your toys. Just cut sections of tubes whatever size you want. Or how about using the small tubes from fabric softener rolls?

Build a house. Just make sure the tubes for the walls are all the same height. Follow the directions for the raft on page 14 to make a roof. Turning the tubes sideways instead of upright will make your house look like a log cabin.

A fence is another thing you can make using shorter tubes.

Great Growers

Cardboard tubes are the perfect shape for vases of all sizes and styles. But we bet you never thought of using tubes as flowerpots. We'll show you how.

You Will Need:

- cardboard tubes
- heavy plastic sandwich bags or other food-storage bags
- rubber bands
- plastic lids
- plastic-foam tray
- various items for decoration: colored paper, ribbon, yarn, buttons
- paint, crayons, markers
- scissors
- glue
- grass and herb seeds
- small plants
- potting soil

To Make the Basic Holder

1 Choose a cardboard tube sized to fit your plan. Decorate it with paint, crayons, or markers, or wrap it with colored paper. We explain exactly how we decorated ours in the steps on these pages.

2 Make a fringe at the bottom of the tube by making cuts in the tube about ½" long and spacing the cuts ¼" to ½" apart. Fan the pieces out. You might need to fold them out and up to form a crease. Glue the fanned-out sections to a plastic lid or plastic-foam tray. Looking at our pictures will help.

3 Open a plastic bag and push it down through the tube. The bag's bottom should rest on the tray or lid. Some of the plastic bag should be sticking out of the top of the tube. Fold that over, then wrap a rubber band around the top twice to hold the bag in place. Trim away any excess plastic.

4 Fill the bag with dampened potting soil. (Spreading it out on a paper plate and sprinkling it with water will probably work best.) After you plant your seeds or plants, water often and carefully. Make sure the soil isn't too wet—your seeds and plants will rot. Plants need sun, too, so find just the right spot—not too cold or too hot.

In addition to tubes, you'll need to gather some seeds and/or seedlings. And don't forget your "green thumb."

To Make the Herb Garden

We used tubes of three different sizes on a plastic-foam tray. You can use a larger tray and more tubes if you want to plant several kinds of herbs. We covered our tray with patches of cut tissue paper and then painted it with a clear varnish. Plant herbs such as mint, parsley, chives, basil, or thyme. You might even try growing a tomato plant. When your plants outgrow the pots, transfer them to a plot outdoors.

To Make the Flowerpot

We spatter painted our tube and used a plastic-lid base. Then we added some decorative ribbon. We put in some silk flowers just to show you how pretty the ones you plant will look. Plant a few wildflower seeds or dried beans. You might even try a tulip or daffodil bulb. Certainly you can plant a small petunia or marigold. Don't forget the sun and water.

To Make the Grass Head

We made ours look like a person. We painted the bottom part of the tube red, added buttons, and topped it with blue ribbon. We used a marker to make the nose and mouth and glued on plastic moveable eyes. We attached our guy to a plastic lid and then "fed" him some soil, grass seed, and water. Soon he had a head of tall, green, grassy hair.

More Ideas

There are dozens of ways to decorate your pots. Try to make them look like clay or decorate them with drawings or stickers. Or make one for a special person, featuring his or her name or initials. Covering the tube with a light coating of glue and wrapping it in yarn or ribbon will make a pretty pot.

Give your grassy-head guy some arms and legs.

Make a pretend fishbowl. Cut a section out of the side of the tube. Put in the plastic bag filled with water and a plastic floating fish. Or attach a tiny toy fish to fishing line and tape the line to the tube. Position the fish so it shows through the opening.

Tubeful Bouquets

The shape of a cardboard tube makes it a natural holder for flowers. Choose one of these and sit it on a table, hang it in a window, or display it on the wall.

You Will Need:

- cardboard tube
- cardboard or foam board
- yarn or ribbon
- dried or silk flowers
- paint or colored paper
- scissors
- glue or tape

To Make the Basic Vase

Choose the flowers you want to display and then pick your cardboard tube according to the size vase you want to make. Decorate it with paint or cover with paper.

To Make the Hanging Bouquet

Make the basic tube. We painted ours with metallic shades of paints. Cover the bottom of the tube with a paper circle or insert the bottom of a paper cup. Punch two holes near the top of the tube and tie on a piece of ribbon or yarn. Arrange flowers, hang, and enjoy.

To Make the Tabletop Bouquet

Make the basic vase. We sponge painted ours. Cut a base from thick cardboard or foam board and decorate it with paper or paint. We made a square, but you can design your own. How about a flower shape? Glue the tube to the base and let it dry. Remember lots of glue needs time to set. Arrange your flowers in the tube.

To Make the Wall Bouquet

Choose your tube and then decorate it. We painted ours with pretty swirls. Hold the tube horizontally, punch holes near its ends, and make a ribbon hanger. Glue or tape flowers in each end. Add a ribbon bow.

More Ideas

Make an apple tree. Decorate the vase like a tree trunk. Use chenille sticks for branches and paper or pompons for apples. In fact, you can make a fruit orchard—lemon, lime, orange, grapefuit, peach, pear, cherry.

Bangles and Bracelets

Plain or fancy—you can make them, wear them, or give them.

You Will Need:

- cardboard tubes
- wrapping paper
- scissors
- glue
- various items for decoration: yarn, lace, paint, glitter, aluminum foil, permanent markers

1 Find a tube large enough to fit over your hand. Decide how wide you want your bracelets to be, and ask an adult to help you cut. Slightly pinching the tube to get started will help.

2 Decorate. We made one curvy and covered it with foil and painted-on designs. We wrapped another in yarn. (Just secure the ends of the yarn with glue.) We painted two others, rolled one in glitter, and glued lace to another.

More Ideas

Have a bracelet-making party. Then give them to residents of an elder-care center. You'll brighten their day and yours.

Use smaller tubes to make bracelets for dolls. Have your friends bring their dolls over and have fun making and exchanging bracelets.

Tube Barrettes

More great crafts to make and wear. And they make gift-giving a snap.

1 Cut sections from a tube. Tubes that are 2" or 3" in diameter work best. Cut each section in half to form two half circles. Decorate. We used printed fabric, felt, and paper.

2 Paint an ice-cream stick. With an adult's help, cut two slits in the barrette. Our pictures show where to put the slits. Make them just wide enough for the stick to fit through. Insert the stick.

More Ideas

Make a set of barrettes for the year's holidays. Use stickers or drawings of valentines, bunnies, ghosts, pumpkins, Pilgrims, Santa, and ideas of your own.

You Will Need:

- cardboard tubes
- ice-cream stick
- various items for decoration, such as paint, fabric, paper, ribbon, rickrack

Winged Wonders

Flutter like a butterfly, buzz like a bee, act like an angel, and sail with the swans—or at least pretend to as you make and enjoy these crafts.

You Will Need:

- cardboard tubes
- paint, crayons, markers
- construction paper
- paper plates
- coffee filters
- cardboard or foam board
- waxed paper
- string or yarn
- various items for decoration
- scissors
- glue

1 Choose the winged wonder you want to make. If it's one of ours, read the directions now. You'll see that the materials needed vary quite a bit. Even the types of tubes that will work best differ. For example, you'll need a very sturdy one for the angel, and a long, somewhat flexible one is required for the swan. If you're crafting a design of your own, get your plan set before you begin.

2 Now you're ready to gather all your materials. Then decorate the cardboard tubes. You can paint them—acrylic paint works best, and it may take more than one coat to cover well enough. Another alternative is to cover them with paper or fabric. Sometimes we paint, color, or draw designs on the paper. It's best to do that before gluing the paper to the tube.

To Make the Butterfly

Punch two holes in your long decorated tube (ours is covered with black paper). These holes are for arms and ours are about 3" from the top of the tube. Decorate flexible paper plates. We used eight dessert-sized ones. Overlap and glue them together as shown. Then glue them to the back of the tube. Insert chenille sticks in the arm holes. Add moveable plastic eyes and chenille-stick antennae. Wow!

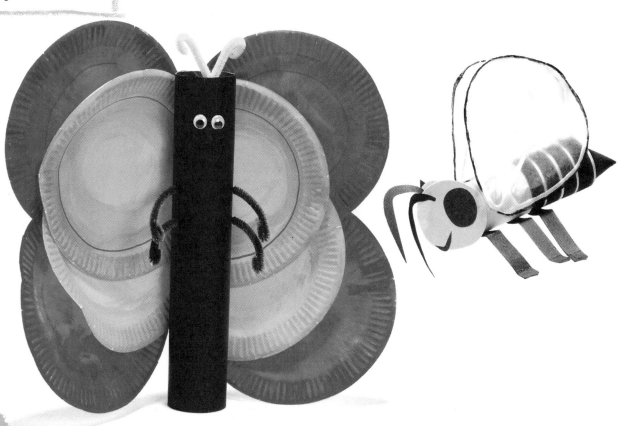

Butterflies, bees, angels, and swans have more in common than wings—they can be crafted from cardboard tubes! These creatures will add beauty to your surroundings.

To Make the Bee

How did you decorate the tube? We covered ours with yellow paper and then added four strips of black construction paper. If you intend to hang your bee, punch holes at each end of the tube now. You'll insert the thread or yarn last. Make a head with facial features and then add antennae, legs, and a cone-shaped stinger. Ours are all from construction paper. Make waxed-paper wings. Outlining them with glue will help them stand up. You can also use glue to show the wing sections. Attach the wings and let your bee buzz away.

To Make the Angel

Did you make the tube angel look special? We did. We painted on a blue dress with a rickrack collar. For her shy face, we used pinkish paper and added details with colored pencils and marker. We cut her hair from yellow paper and wrapped and glued it around her head. Then we added a golden halo made from garland. Her arms are paper. Her cape and wings are made from ripply coffee filters. We colored the edges, folded the filters in half, and then overlapped them as shown. Once the wings are attached, make sure she doesn't fly away!

To Make the Swan

You'll need two tubes, a long flexible one and a shorter sturdy one. Start by attaching the sturdy one to a rectangle of cardboard. Bend your long tube into a Z shape as you can see in our picture. Place the bottom of the Z into the sturdy tube and attach with tape or glue. Paint some flexible paper plates. We overlapped one salad-sized and five dinner-sized plates for each wing. Make a beak from lightweight cardboard, add eyes and pompon details. Sail away!

More Ideas

There are all kinds of winged things you can make using tubes as bodies and creating wings from a variety of materials. Try your hand at an eagle, a turkey, a peacock, a Halloween bat, or a fairy godmother.

Make a host of angels to decorate your holiday mantel or table. Making a variety of sizes will add interest.

Someone you know probably collects butterflies and/or angels. Now you can add to their collection with a hand-crafted one.

Tube Frame

What a perfect—and easy—way to present those special photos or original artwork!

You Will Need:
- cardboard tubes
- plastic-foam tray
- scissors
- glue
- various items for decoration

1 Choose the photo you want to showcase and then choose the right-sized tubes. We used bathroom tissue tubes. Decorate and then starting at the top, slit the tubes. Stop at least 1" from the bottom.

2 Paint and/or decorate the tray. We cut ours to make it look like a short table. Glue the tubes in place, placing them just far enough apart for your picture to fit. Insert your picture and make someone happy.

More Ideas

Gluing the photo or artwork to lightweight cardboard will help hold the frame's shape. You may need to enlarge the slits a little. Also, laminating or covering the photo with plastic wrap or stiff, clear plastic will help protect it.

O'Deer

Is it a centerpiece, an ornament, a puppet, or a friend? It can be all these and more.

You Will Need:
- cardboard tube
- construction paper
- twigs
- scissors
- glue
- various items for decoration

1 Cut four sections from the bottom of the tube to form the deer's legs. We added black paper hooves.

2 Add facial features. Be as creative as you dare. We used a Rudolph pompon nose and then added a ribbon with a bell.

3 Punch a hole on each side of the reindeer's head and insert "twig" antlers.

More Ideas

Make a herd of deer. Use them as finger puppets and create a play that you can perform for family and friends.

Hobby Tube Zebra

Don't you know a child who would just love a hobby horse-type toy? Have fun making one—or two! Then enjoy the scene as your little friend rides all around.

You Will Need:

- cardboard tube
- cereal box
- paint, crayons, markers
- construction paper or lightweight cardboard
- ribbon, yarn, or heavy string
- scissors
- glue or tape

More Ideas

Obviously you can make a hobby tube animal of any sort. How about a mustang mare, a long-necked giraffe, a back-packing camel, or a surprising ostrich?

Your hobby-horselike toy doesn't have to be an animal. It can be a cartoon or movie character.

Make small versions of these crafts to hang as wall decorations in a toddler's room. Or how about this for a challenge: Make really tiny ones and hang them from a paper-plate mobile.

1 Decide what toy you want to make. Will you make a zebra or some other toy? Decorate a long wrapping paper tube—ours is 32" long. (You can always put shorter tubes together with strong tape.) We began with a 4' x 32" piece of white paper, painted on black stripes, and covered the tube.

2 Make the head from a cereal box. Ask an adult for help in cutting out a wedge. Looking at our picture will show the shape you need. For the neck part of the head, leave the bottom of the box in place and cut out a circle the size of your tube. We covered our box with heavy black paper. (Heavy paper or lightweight cardboard covers the openings well.) Make the paper about ¼" longer than the neck.

3 We cut out and glued "stripes" of white paper to the black-paper head. Next we added an eye, pink-lined black ears, and two sections of pink-fringed mane. It's easy to attach the mane if you first cut a piece that is double the shape you want. Fringe on both sides and fold up both sides, leaving a 1" flat strip down the middle. Glue that flat strip in place. Our final touches were a pink paper nose and a pink paper-and-ribbon harness.

4 Slide the tube all the way up into the box. If the circle you cut in Step 2 isn't too big, the tube will probably stay in just fine. Otherwise, add glue or tape. Your toy is finally ready to ride!

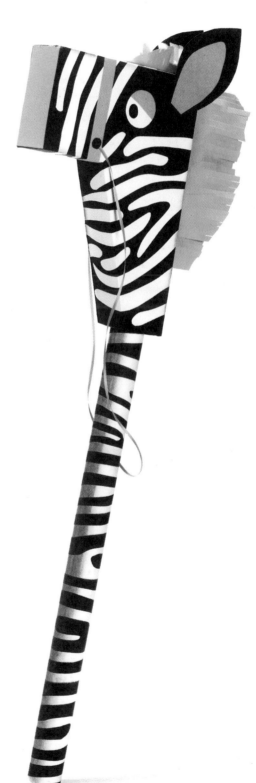

Title Index

Subject Index